CHEF LEGENDS ALPHABET

Words by Robin Feiner

Aa

A is for **A**nthony Bourdain. The original celebrity TV chef who, in 2002, changed cooking shows from 'stand and stir' to the documentary-style cultural discoveries that became his signature. His legendary love of food was the spice for his storytelling.

Bb

B is for Massimo Bottura. They say you should never mess with nonna's recipes, but this 3-starred Italian maverick blended tradition with originality, and reinvented Italian cuisine! His new sustainability movement challenges chefs around the world to get creative about reducing food waste.

C is for Cat Cora.
With her growing empire of restaurants, cookbooks and TV shows, the world's first female Iron Chef dominates in a traditionally male industry. She also serves up 'Chefs for Humanity,' a program that helps fight obesity and hunger in the U.S.

D is for **D**avid Chang. Pork buns, fried Brussels sprouts, and a no-nonsense, rebellious vibe. The Korean American genius behind 'Momofuku' and 'Ugly Delicious' turned fine dining on its head and transformed the culture of food. Chang is all about change!

E is for Auguste **E**scoffier. This 19th-century French restauranteur literally wrote the textbook on being a chef: 'Le Guide Culinaire.' The King of Chefs also invented à la carte dining and revolutionized the way kitchens are run – a legacy that still lives on today.

Ff

F is for **F**erran Adrià.
Chef or scientist? This Spanish culinary wizard became controversial for deconstructing his ingredients on a molecular level, radically changing their form while maintaining their burst of flavor. His restaurant 'El Bulli' was named best eatery in the world many times.

G is for **G**ordon Ramsay. Training under culinary masters Albert Roux, Marco Pierre White, Guy Savoy and Joël Robuchon, this British livewire burst onto TV screens and became a household name. His constellation of Michelin stars proves his cuisine is as hot as his temper!

H is for Heston Blumenthal. Like Ferran Adrià, Blumenthal captured the world's attention with his mathematical approach to preparing dishes. He's the mad scientist behind bizarre combos like bacon and egg ice cream, and snail porridge, and flavor explosions like triple-cooked chips!

I is for Irma S. Rombauer. In 1936, this American socialite published one of the most popular cookbooks ever: 'Joy of Cooking.' It was her chatty side notes and anecdotes that made the cookbook – and cooking itself – such a delight for readers.

BON APPÉTIT

Jj

J is for Julia Child.
She's the American cook
who fell in love with French
cuisine and revolutionized
home cooking in America.
Her TV show, 'The French
Chef,' always included a
dollop of her hearty humor!
"A party without cake is
just a meeting."

K is for Ken Hom.
Beloved by the public
and his peers alike, this
Chinese American author,
TV presenter and master of
Asian cuisine single-handedly
introduced Chinese food to
the U.K. The Wok Wizard
even invented the flat-
bottomed wok to fit on
British stoves! Legend.

L is for Edna Lewis.
With a deep love and respect for her country roots, the Grande Dame of Southern Cooking honored the traditional harvesting, preparation and cooking methods of the South, elevating its cuisine, and inspiring an entire generation of young chefs.

M is for **M**asaharu Morimoto. Japanese aromas, Chinese spices, Italian ingredients and French presentation. Slicing and dicing his way through exhilarating culinary battles on 'Iron Chef,' this cutting-edge Japanese chef blends East and West flavors like no other.

N is for **N**igella Lawson. Starting out as a food journalist and cookbook author, the Domestic Goddess became an instant hit with TV audiences all over the world for her simple, appetite-driven dishes and her relaxed, confident vibe in the kitchen.

O is for Jamie Oliver.
The Naked Chef burst onto
the scene as an unpretentious
fresh-faced lad who spoke
and cooked so casually,
it made expert cooking
achievable for the average
family. His campaign for
healthier eating literally
changed lunch menus in
British schools.

P is for Anne-Sophie Pic.
As only the fourth female
chef with three Michelin stars,
the queen of French cuisine
brings a sense of grace and
elegance to the table. Her
cuisine is poetic and musical,
a harmonious balance of
flavors and emotion.

Qq

Q is for Queen of Cake:
Sylvia Weinstock. Whether
she's baking for Hollywood
royalty or the bride next door,
this legendary New York
baker and cake designer's
confectionary is a work
of art. Every creation is
a delicious, handcrafted
buttercream dream.

R is for **R**achael Ray.
"We'll see you when we
see you." She's the popular
American celebrity cook and
talk show host who whips
up quick and easy meals that
anyone can recreate at home.
Her non-profit organization
'Yum-O!' encourages healthy
relationships with food.

S is for Clare Smyth. This classically trained Northern Irish chef was the first female to run a British restaurant with three Michelin stars. Since then, she's received multiple Best Chef accolades, and even cooked for Prince Harry and Meghan Markle's wedding!

T is for Christina **T**osi. The cherry atop David Chang's foodie empire, Tosi is the cookie queen behind the 'Momofuku Milk Bar' restaurants. With a passion for all things sweet and gooey, her compost cookies and cereal milk soft serve ice cream are global sensations!

U is for Louis Eustache Ude. This pompous French culinary artist was chef to royalty and diplomats like King Louis XVI and Napoleon Bonaparte's mother. It's rumored he resigned as chef to Britain's Earl of Sefton when a guest dared to add salt to the soup!

V is for Vivek Singh.
After a stellar career in India,
Singh moved to London to
open his now-renowned first
restaurant, 'The Cinnamon
Club.' Reimagining dishes
from his native India, his
cuisine is both "new and old,
east and west, the best of
all worlds."

W is for Wolfgang Puck. He's the Austrian American revolutionary who brought fine dining to the U.S. in the 1980s when he opened his famed Italian-style trattoria, 'Spago.' Today, his name is internationally synonymous with the best in culinary arts. Legend!

Xx

X is for Xavier Marcel Boulestin. Before Bourdain, there was Boulestin, the cosmopolitan French chef who was a breath of fresh air as host of Britain's 'Cook's Night Out' in the 1930s. His perfect omelet is considered the first dish ever cooked on TV!

Y is for Yotam Ottolenghi. He's the world's most famous non-vegetarian vegetarian cookbook author! With one single lemon on the cover of his best-seller, this Israeli English chef's philosophy is to let the ingredients do the talking. "I want drama in the mouth."

Zz

Z is for Adriano **Z**umbo. Ever since he introduced Australia to the soft, colorful sweetness of macarons, this pastry chef and TV personality has wowed audiences with his weird and wonderful desserts. It's no wonder he's known as Australia's Willy Wonka!